# 75 *Soft*

# *Challenges*

## *for Women*

## PERSONAL INFORMATION

**Name:**

**Address:**

**Phone:**

**Email:**

# 75 Days Soft Challenges

START DATE:

FINISH DATE:

1　2　3　4　5　6　7

8　9　10　11　12　13　14

15　16　17　18　19　20　21

22　23　24　25　26　27　28

29　30　31　32　33　34　35

36　37　38　39　40　41　42

43　44　45　46　47　48　49

50　51　52　53　54　55　56

57　58　59　60　61　62　63

64　65　66　67　68　69　70

71　72　73　74　75　CONGRATULATIONS

# 75 Days Soft Challenges

## GOLDEN RULES

- FOLLOW YOUR DIET
- TAKE A PROGRESS PHOTO
- DRINK 3L WATER EVERYDAY
- READ 10 PAGES DAILY
- DAILY 45-MINUTE WORKOUT

## STARTING POINT

| | | | |
|---|---|---|---|
| STARTING WEIGHT | | DATE : | |
| GOAL WEIGHT | | DATE : | |
| FINAL WEIGHT | | DATE : | |

## MEASUREMENTS

BODY MASS: _____

BODY FAT%: _____

HEIGHT: _____

NECK: _____

SHOULDER: _____

CHEST: _____

WAIST: _____

BELLY: _____

HIP: _____

THIGH: _____

CALF: _____

HEIGHT

NECK

SHOULDER

CHEST

WAIST

BELLY

HIP

THIGH

CALF

## NOTES

_____
_____
_____
_____
_____
_____
_____

# 75 Day Soft Challenge

## WEEKLY MEASURUMENTS

**Week 1**

| | |
|---|---|
| START DAY | |
| START GOAL | |
| FINISH DAY | |
| FINISH GOAL | |

| WEIGHT | ARM | CHEST | WAIST |
|---|---|---|---|
| | | | |

| BELLY | HIP | THIGH | CALF |
|---|---|---|---|
| | | | |

## WEEKLY MEAL PLANNING

| DAY | BREAKFAST | LUNCH | DINNER | SNACKS | TOTAL CAL |
|---|---|---|---|---|---|
| 1 | | | | | |
| 2 | | | | | |
| 3 | | | | | |
| 4 | | | | | |
| 5 | | | | | |
| 6 | | | | | |
| 7 | | | | | |

# 75 Days Soft Challenges

## GROCERY SHOPPING LIST

- ○ _____
- ○ _____
- ○ _____
- ○ _____
- ○ _____
- ○ _____
- ○ _____

- ○ _____
- ○ _____
- ○ _____
- ○ _____
- ○ _____
- ○ _____
- ○ _____

- ○ _____
- ○ _____
- ○ _____
- ○ _____
- ○ _____
- ○ _____
- ○ _____

## NOTES

_____

_____

_____

_____

_____

_____

_____

_____

_____

_____

_____

# 75 Day Soft Challenge

Date: _____    S  M  T  W  T  F  S

## DAY 1

- FOLLOW YOUR DIET ○
- TAKE A PROGRESS PHOTO ○
- DRINK 3L WATER EVERYDAY ○
- READ 10 PAGES DAILY ○
- DAILY 45-MINUTE WORKOUT ○

## REFLECTION OF THE DAY

**Physical Health** _____

**Mental Health** _____

**The Things that Made You Feel Good Today** _____

## DIET STRATEGY

Breakfast _____

Lunch _____

Dinner _____

Snacks _____

## NOTES

## DAILY READING

BOOK TITEL _____

AUTHOR _____

PAGES _____

## WORKOUT PLAN

WORKOUT PLAN 1          WORKOUT PLAN 2

# 75 Day Soft Challenge

**Date:** _____   S  M  T  W  T  F  S

## DAY 2

- FOLLOW YOUR DIET ⭕
- TAKE A PROGRESS PHOTO ⭕
- DRINK 3L WATER EVERYDAY ⭕
- READ 10 PAGES DAILY ⭕
- DAILY 45-MINUTE WORKOUT ⭕

## REFLECTION OF THE DAY

**Physical Health** _____

**Mental Health** _____

**The Things that Made You Feel Good Today** _____

## DIET STRATEGY

Breakfast _____

Lunch _____

Dinner _____

Snacks _____

## NOTES

_____

## DAILY READING

BOOK TITEL _____

AUTHOR _____

PAGES _____

## WORKOUT PLAN

| WORKOUT PLAN 1 | WORKOUT PLAN 2 |
|---|---|
|  |  |

# 75 Day Soft Challenge

Date: _____  **S  M  T  W  T  F  S**

## DAY 3

- FOLLOW YOUR DIET ◯
- TAKE A PROGRESS PHOTO ◯
- DRINK 3L WATER EVERYDAY ◯
- READ 10 PAGES DAILY ◯
- DAILY 45-MINUTE WORKOUT ◯

## REFLECTION OF THE DAY

**Physical Health** _____

**Mental Health** _____

**The Things that Made You Feel Good Today** _____

## DIET STRATEGY

Breakfast _____

Lunch _____

Dinner _____

Snacks _____

## NOTES

## DAILY READING

BOOK TITEL _____

AUTHOR _____

PAGES _____

## WORKOUT PLAN

WORKOUT PLAN 1          WORKOUT PLAN 2

# 75 Day Soft Challenge

Date: _____    S  M  T  W  T  F  S

## DAY
### 4

- FOLLOW YOUR DIET ⃝
- TAKE A PROGRESS PHOTO ⃝
- DRINK 3L WATER EVERYDAY ⃝
- READ 10 PAGES DAILY ⃝
- DAILY 45-MINUTE WORKOUT ⃝

## REFLECTION OF THE DAY

| **Physical Health** | _____ |
| **Mental Health** | _____ |
| The Things that Made You Feel Good Today | _____ |

## DIET STRATEGY

| Breakfast | _____ |
| Lunch | _____ |
| Dinner | _____ |
| Snacks | _____ |

## NOTES

## DAILY READING

| BOOK TITEL | _____ |
| AUTHOR | _____ |
| PAGES | _____ |

## WORKOUT PLAN

| WORKOUT PLAN 1 | WORKOUT PLAN 2 |

# 75 Day Soft Challenge

**Date:** _____    S  M  T  W  T  F  S

## DAY 5

- FOLLOW YOUR DIET ○
- TAKE A PROGRESS PHOTO ○
- DRINK 3L WATER EVERYDAY ○
- READ 10 PAGES DAILY ○
- DAILY 45-MINUTE WORKOUT ○

## REFLECTION OF THE DAY

| **Physical Health** | |
| **Mental Health** | |
| The Things that Made You Feel Good Today | |

## DIET STRATEGY

| Breakfast | |
| Lunch | |
| Dinner | |
| Snacks | |

## NOTES

## DAILY READING

| BOOK TITEL | |
| AUTHOR | |
| PAGES | |

## WORKOUT PLAN

| WORKOUT PLAN 1 | WORKOUT PLAN 2 |
| | |

# 75 Day Soft Challenge

**Date:** _____  S  M  T  W  T  F  S

## DAY
## 6

- FOLLOW YOUR DIET ○
- TAKE A PROGRESS PHOTO ○
- DRINK 3L WATER EVERYDAY ○
- READ 10 PAGES DAILY ○
- DAILY 45-MINUTE WORKOUT ○

## REFLECTION OF THE DAY

| | |
|---|---|
| **Physical Health** | |
| **Mental Health** | |
| The Things that Made You Feel Good Today | |

## DIET STRATEGY

| | |
|---|---|
| Breakfast | |
| Lunch | |
| Dinner | |
| Snacks | |

## NOTES

## DAILY READING

| | |
|---|---|
| BOOK TITEL | |
| AUTHOR | |
| PAGES | |

## WORKOUT PLAN

| WORKOUT PLAN 1 | WORKOUT PLAN 2 |
|---|---|
| | |

# 75 Day Soft Challenge

Date: _____    **S M T W T F S**

## DAY 7

- FOLLOW YOUR DIET ○
- TAKE A PROGRESS PHOTO ○
- DRINK 3L WATER EVERYDAY ○
- READ 10 PAGES DAILY ○
- DAILY 45-MINUTE WORKOUT ○

## REFLECTION OF THE DAY

**Physical Health** _____

**Mental Health** _____

**The Things that Made You Feel Good Today** _____

## DIET STRATEGY

Breakfast _____

Lunch _____

Dinner _____

Snacks _____

## NOTES

## DAILY READING

BOOK TITEL _____
AUTHOR _____
PAGES _____

## WORKOUT PLAN

WORKOUT PLAN 1    WORKOUT PLAN 2

# 75 Days Soft Challenges

## NOTES

# 75 Days Soft Challenges

## WEEKLY MEASURUMENTS

**Week 2**

| | |
|---|---|
| START DAY | |
| START GOAL | |
| FINISH DAY | |
| FINISH GOAL | |

| WEIGHT | ARM | CHEST | WAIST |
|---|---|---|---|
| | | | |

| BELLY | HIP | THIGH | CALF |
|---|---|---|---|
| | | | |

## WEEKLY MEAL PLANNING

| DAY | BREAKFAST | LUNCH | DINNER | SNACKS | TOTAL CAL |
|---|---|---|---|---|---|
| 1 | | | | | |
| 2 | | | | | |
| 3 | | | | | |
| 4 | | | | | |
| 5 | | | | | |
| 6 | | | | | |
| 7 | | | | | |

# 75 Days Soft Challenges

## GROCERY SHOPPING LIST

- ○ _____
- ○ _____
- ○ _____
- ○ _____
- ○ _____
- ○ _____
- ○ _____

- ○ _____
- ○ _____
- ○ _____
- ○ _____
- ○ _____
- ○ _____
- ○ _____

- ○ _____
- ○ _____
- ○ _____
- ○ _____
- ○ _____
- ○ _____
- ○ _____

## NOTES

_____

_____

_____

_____

_____

_____

_____

_____

_____

_____

_____

_____

_____

# 75 Day Soft Challenge

**Date:** _____  S M T W T F S

## DAY 8

- FOLLOW YOUR DIET ○
- TAKE A PROGRESS PHOTO ○
- DRINK 3L WATER EVERYDAY ○
- READ 10 PAGES DAILY ○
- DAILY 45-MINUTE WORKOUT ○

## REFLECTION OF THE DAY

**Physical Health** _____

**Mental Health** _____

**The Things that Made You Feel Good Today** _____

## DIET STRATEGY

Breakfast _____

Lunch _____

Dinner _____

Snacks _____

## NOTES

_____

## DAILY READING

BOOK TITEL _____

AUTHOR _____

PAGES _____

## WORKOUT PLAN

WORKOUT PLAN 1

WORKOUT PLAN 2

# 75 Day Soft Challenge

Date: _____  **S  M  T  W  T  F  S**

## DAY
## 9

- FOLLOW YOUR DIET ◯
- TAKE A PROGRESS PHOTO ◯
- DRINK 3L WATER EVERYDAY ◯
- READ 10 PAGES DAILY ◯
- DAILY 45-MINUTE WORKOUT ◯

## REFLECTION OF THE DAY

| **Physical Health** | |
| **Mental Health** | |
| The Things that Made You Feel Good Today | |

## DIET STRATEGY

| Breakfast | |
| Lunch | |
| Dinner | |
| Snacks | |

## NOTES

## DAILY READING

| BOOK TITEL | |
| AUTHOR | |
| PAGES | |

## WORKOUT PLAN

| WORKOUT PLAN 1 | WORKOUT PLAN 2 |
| | |

# 75 Day Soft Challenge

Date: _____    **S M T W T F S**

## DAY
## 10

- FOLLOW YOUR DIET  ◯
- TAKE A PROGRESS PHOTO  ◯
- DRINK 3L WATER EVERYDAY  ◯
- READ 10 PAGES DAILY  ◯
- DAILY 45-MINUTE WORKOUT  ◯

## REFLECTION OF THE DAY

| **Physical Health** | _____ |
| **Mental Health** | _____ |
| The Things that Made You Feel Good Today | _____ |

## DIET STRATEGY

| Breakfast | _____ |
| Lunch | _____ |
| Dinner | _____ |
| Snacks | _____ |

## NOTES

## DAILY READING

BOOK TITEL
AUTHOR
PAGES

## WORKOUT PLAN

| WORKOUT PLAN 1 | WORKOUT PLAN 2 |

# 75 Day Soft Challenge

Date: _____  **S  M  T  W  T  F  S**

## DAY
## 11

- FOLLOW YOUR DIET ○
- TAKE A PROGRESS PHOTO ○
- DRINK 3L WATER EVERYDAY ○
- READ 10 PAGES DAILY ○
- DAILY 45-MINUTE WORKOUT ○

## REFLECTION OF THE DAY

| **Physical Health** | |
| --- | --- |
| **Mental Health** | |
| The Things that Made You Feel Good Today | |

## DIET STRATEGY

| Breakfast | |
| --- | --- |
| Lunch | |
| Dinner | |
| Snacks | |

## NOTES

## DAILY READING

| BOOK TITEL | |
| --- | --- |
| AUTHOR | |
| PAGES | |

## WORKOUT PLAN

| WORKOUT PLAN 1 | WORKOUT PLAN 2 |
| --- | --- |
| | |

# 75 Day Soft Challenge

Date: _____  **S M T W T F S**

## DAY
## 12

- FOLLOW YOUR DIET ○
- TAKE A PROGRESS PHOTO ○
- DRINK 3L WATER EVERYDAY ○
- READ 10 PAGES DAILY ○
- DAILY 45-MINUTE WORKOUT ○

## REFLECTION OF THE DAY

**Physical Health**
_____
_____
_____

**Mental Health**
_____
_____
_____

**The Things that Made You Feel Good Today**
_____
_____
_____

## DIET STRATEGY

Breakfast
_____
_____

Lunch
_____
_____

Dinner
_____
_____

Snacks
_____
_____

## NOTES

## DAILY READING

BOOK TITEL _____
AUTHOR _____
PAGES _____

## WORKOUT PLAN

WORKOUT PLAN 1     WORKOUT PLAN 2

# 75 Day Soft Challenge

Date: _____

**S M T W T F S**

## DAY 13

- FOLLOW YOUR DIET ○
- TAKE A PROGRESS PHOTO ○
- DRINK 3L WATER EVERYDAY ○
- READ 10 PAGES DAILY ○
- DAILY 45-MINUTE WORKOUT ○

## REFLECTION OF THE DAY

**Physical Health**
_____
_____

**Mental Health**
_____
_____

**The Things that Made You Feel Good Today**
_____
_____

## DIET STRATEGY

Breakfast
_____
_____

Lunch
_____
_____

Dinner
_____
_____

Snacks
_____
_____

## NOTES

## DAILY READING

BOOK TITEL
AUTHOR
PAGES

## WORKOUT PLAN

WORKOUT PLAN 1

WORKOUT PLAN 2

# 75 Day Soft Challenge

Date: _____    S  M  T  W  T  F  S

## DAY
## 14

- 🍴 FOLLOW YOUR DIET ⭕
- 📷 TAKE A PROGRESS PHOTO ⭕
- 🧴 DRINK 3L WATER EVERYDAY ⭕
- 📖 READ 10 PAGES DAILY ⭕
- 🏋️ DAILY 45-MINUTE WORKOUT ⭕

## REFLECTION OF THE DAY

| **Physical Health** | _____ |
| **Mental Health** | _____ |
| **The Things that Made You Feel Good Today** | _____ |

## DIET STRATEGY

| Breakfast | _____ |
| Lunch | _____ |
| Dinner | _____ |
| Snacks | _____ |

## NOTES

## DAILY READING

- BOOK TITEL _____
- AUTHOR _____
- PAGES _____

## WORKOUT PLAN

| WORKOUT PLAN 1 | WORKOUT PLAN 2 |

# 75 Days Soft Challenges

## NOTES

# 75 Days Soft Challenges

## WEEKLY MEASURUMENTS

**Week 3**

| | |
|---|---|
| START DAY | _____ |
| START GOAL | _____ |
| FINISH DAY | _____ |
| FINISH GOAL | _____ |

| WEIGHT | ARM | CHEST | WAIST |
|---|---|---|---|
| | | | |

| BELLY | HIP | THIGH | CALF |
|---|---|---|---|
| | | | |

## WEEKLY MEAL PLANNING

| DAY | BREAKFAST | LUNCH | DINNER | SNACKS | TOTAL CAL |
|---|---|---|---|---|---|
| 1 | | | | | |
| 2 | | | | | |
| 3 | | | | | |
| 4 | | | | | |
| 5 | | | | | |
| 6 | | | | | |
| 7 | | | | | |

# 75 Days Soft Challenges

## GROCERY SHOPPING LIST

- ◯ _____
- ◯ _____
- ◯ _____
- ◯ _____
- ◯ _____
- ◯ _____
- ◯ _____

- ◯ _____
- ◯ _____
- ◯ _____
- ◯ _____
- ◯ _____
- ◯ _____
- ◯ _____

- ◯ _____
- ◯ _____
- ◯ _____
- ◯ _____
- ◯ _____
- ◯ _____
- ◯ _____

## NOTES

_____

_____

_____

_____

_____

_____

_____

_____

_____

_____

_____

_____

# 75 Day Soft Challenge

Date: _____  **S  M  T  W  T  F  S**

## DAY
## 15

- FOLLOW YOUR DIET ○
- TAKE A PROGRESS PHOTO ○
- DRINK 3L WATER EVERYDAY ○
- READ 10 PAGES DAILY ○
- DAILY 45-MINUTE WORKOUT ○

## REFLECTION OF THE DAY

| **Physical Health** | _____ |
| **Mental Health** | _____ |
| The Things that Made You Feel Good Today | _____ |

## DIET STRATEGY

| Breakfast | _____ |
| Lunch | _____ |
| Dinner | _____ |
| Snacks | _____ |

## NOTES

## DAILY READING

BOOK TITEL  _____
AUTHOR  _____
PAGES  _____

## WORKOUT PLAN

| WORKOUT PLAN 1 | WORKOUT PLAN 2 |

# 75 Day Soft Challenge

Date: _____    S   M   T   W   T   F   S

## DAY
## 16

- 🍴 FOLLOW YOUR DIET ⃝
- 📷 TAKE A PROGRESS PHOTO ⃝
- 📱 DRINK 3L WATER EVERYDAY ⃝
- 📖 READ 10 PAGES DAILY ⃝
- 🏋 DAILY 45-MINUTE WORKOUT ⃝

## REFLECTION OF THE DAY

| **Physical Health** | _____ |
| **Mental Health** | _____ |
| The Things that Made You Feel Good Today | _____ |

## DIET STRATEGY

| Breakfast | _____ |
| Lunch | _____ |
| Dinner | _____ |
| Snacks | _____ |

## NOTES

## DAILY READING

BOOK TITEL _____
AUTHOR _____
PAGES _____

## WORKOUT PLAN

| WORKOUT PLAN 1 | WORKOUT PLAN 2 |

# 75 Day Soft Challenge

Date: _____   **S  M  T  W  T  F  S**

## DAY
## 17

- FOLLOW YOUR DIET ○
- TAKE A PROGRESS PHOTO ○
- DRINK 3L WATER EVERYDAY ○
- READ 10 PAGES DAILY ○
- DAILY 45-MINUTE WORKOUT ○

## REFLECTION OF THE DAY

| **Physical Health** | |
| **Mental Health** | |
| The Things that Made You Feel Good Today | |

## DIET STRATEGY

| Breakfast | |
| Lunch | |
| Dinner | |
| Snacks | |

## NOTES

## DAILY READING

| BOOK TITEL | |
| AUTHOR | |
| PAGES | |

## WORKOUT PLAN

| WORKOUT PLAN 1 | WORKOUT PLAN 2 |

# 75 Day Soft Challenge

Date: _____   S  M  T  W  T  F  S

## DAY 18

- FOLLOW YOUR DIET
- TAKE A PROGRESS PHOTO
- DRINK 3L WATER EVERYDAY
- READ 10 PAGES DAILY
- DAILY 45-MINUTE WORKOUT

## REFLECTION OF THE DAY

**Physical Health**
_____
_____

**Mental Health**
_____
_____

**The Things that Made You Feel Good Today**
_____
_____

## NOTES

## DIET STRATEGY

Breakfast
_____
_____

Lunch
_____
_____

Dinner
_____
_____

Snacks
_____
_____

## DAILY READING

BOOK TITEL
AUTHOR
PAGES

## WORKOUT PLAN

WORKOUT PLAN 1      WORKOUT PLAN 2

# 75 Day Soft Challenge

Date: _____  **S M T W T F S**

## DAY
## 19

- FOLLOW YOUR DIET ○
- TAKE A PROGRESS PHOTO ○
- DRINK 3L WATER EVERYDAY ○
- READ 10 PAGES DAILY ○
- DAILY 45-MINUTE WORKOUT ○

## REFLECTION OF THE DAY

| **Physical Health** | |
| **Mental Health** | |
| The Things that Made You Feel Good Today | |

## DIET STRATEGY

| Breakfast | |
| Lunch | |
| Dinner | |
| Snacks | |

## NOTES

## DAILY READING

| BOOK TITEL | |
| AUTHOR | |
| PAGES | |

## WORKOUT PLAN

| WORKOUT PLAN 1 | WORKOUT PLAN 2 |

# 75 Day Soft Challenge

Date: _____  **S   M   T   W   T   F   S**

## DAY
## 20

- FOLLOW YOUR DIET ○
- TAKE A PROGRESS PHOTO ○
- DRINK 3L WATER EVERYDAY ○
- READ 10 PAGES DAILY ○
- DAILY 45-MINUTE WORKOUT ○

## REFLECTION OF THE DAY

| | |
|---|---|
| **Physical Health** | |
| **Mental Health** | |
| **The Things that Made You Feel Good Today** | |

## DIET STRATEGY

| | |
|---|---|
| Breakfast | |
| Lunch | |
| Dinner | |
| Snacks | |

## NOTES

## DAILY READING

| BOOK TITEL | |
|---|---|
| AUTHOR | |
| PAGES | |

## WORKOUT PLAN

| WORKOUT PLAN 1 | WORKOUT PLAN 2 |
|---|---|
| | |

# 75 Day Soft Challenge

Date: _____  **S  M  T  W  T  F  S**

## DAY 21

- FOLLOW YOUR DIET ◯
- TAKE A PROGRESS PHOTO ◯
- DRINK 3L WATER EVERYDAY ◯
- READ 10 PAGES DAILY ◯
- DAILY 45-MINUTE WORKOUT ◯

## REFLECTION OF THE DAY

**Physical Health** | _____

**Mental Health** | _____

**The Things that Made You Feel Good Today** | _____

## DIET STRATEGY

Breakfast | _____

Lunch | _____

Dinner | _____

Snacks | _____

## NOTES

## DAILY READING

BOOK TITEL | _____
AUTHOR | _____
PAGES | _____

## WORKOUT PLAN

WORKOUT PLAN 1 | WORKOUT PLAN 2

# 75 Days Soft Challenges

## NOTES

# 75 Days Soft Challenges

## WEEKLY MEASURUMENTS

**Week 4**

| | |
|---|---|
| START DAY | |
| START GOAL | |
| FINISH DAY | |
| FINISH GOAL | |

| WEIGHT | ARM | CHEST | WAIST |
|---|---|---|---|
| | | | |

| BELLY | HIP | THIGH | CALF |
|---|---|---|---|
| | | | |

## WEEKLY MEAL PLANNING

| DAY | BREAKFAST | LUNCH | DINNER | SNACKS | TOTAL CAL |
|---|---|---|---|---|---|
| 1 | | | | | |
| 2 | | | | | |
| 3 | | | | | |
| 4 | | | | | |
| 5 | | | | | |
| 6 | | | | | |
| 7 | | | | | |

# 75 Days Soft Challenges

## GROCERY SHOPPING LIST

- ◯ _____
- ◯ _____
- ◯ _____
- ◯ _____
- ◯ _____
- ◯ _____
- ◯ _____

- ◯ _____
- ◯ _____
- ◯ _____
- ◯ _____
- ◯ _____
- ◯ _____
- ◯ _____

- ◯ _____
- ◯ _____
- ◯ _____
- ◯ _____
- ◯ _____
- ◯ _____
- ◯ _____

## NOTES

_____

_____

_____

_____

_____

_____

_____

_____

_____

_____

_____

_____

# 75 Day Soft Challenge

Date: _____    S  M  T  W  T  F  S

## DAY 22

- 🍴 FOLLOW YOUR DIET ⭕
- 📷 TAKE A PROGRESS PHOTO ⭕
- 📱 DRINK 3L WATER EVERYDAY ⭕
- 📖 READ 10 PAGES DAILY ⭕
- 🏋 DAILY 45-MINUTE WORKOUT ⭕

## REFLECTION OF THE DAY

| Physical Health | _____ |
| Mental Health | _____ |
| The Things that Made You Feel Good Today | _____ |

## DIET STRATEGY

| Breakfast | _____ |
| Lunch | _____ |
| Dinner | _____ |
| Snacks | _____ |

## NOTES

## DAILY READING

- BOOK TITEL _____
- AUTHOR _____
- PAGES _____

## WORKOUT PLAN

| WORKOUT PLAN 1 | WORKOUT PLAN 2 |

# 75 Day Soft Challenge

Date: _____  **S M T W T F S**

**DAY**
## 23

- FOLLOW YOUR DIET ◯
- TAKE A PROGRESS PHOTO ◯
- DRINK 3L WATER EVERYDAY ◯
- READ 10 PAGES DAILY ◯
- DAILY 45-MINUTE WORKOUT ◯

## REFLECTION OF THE DAY

**Physical Health**

**Mental Health**

**The Things that Made You Feel Good Today**

## DIET STRATEGY

Breakfast

Lunch

Dinner

Snacks

## NOTES

## DAILY READING

BOOK TITEL

AUTHOR

PAGES

## WORKOUT PLAN

WORKOUT PLAN 1

WORKOUT PLAN 2

# 75 Day Soft Challenge

Date: _____  **S M T W T F S**

## DAY 24

- FOLLOW YOUR DIET
- TAKE A PROGRESS PHOTO
- DRINK 3L WATER EVERYDAY
- READ 10 PAGES DAILY
- DAILY 45-MINUTE WORKOUT

## REFLECTION OF THE DAY

**Physical Health**

**Mental Health**

**The Things that Made You Feel Good Today**

## DIET STRATEGY

Breakfast

Lunch

Dinner

Snacks

## NOTES

## DAILY READING

BOOK TITEL

AUTHOR

PAGES

## WORKOUT PLAN

WORKOUT PLAN 1

WORKOUT PLAN 2

# 75 Day Soft Challenge

Date: _____    S  M  T  W  T  F  S

**DAY**
## 25

- 🍴 FOLLOW YOUR DIET ◯
- 📷 TAKE A PROGRESS PHOTO ◯
- 📱 DRINK 3L WATER EVERYDAY ◯
- 📖 READ 10 PAGES DAILY ◯
- 🏋 DAILY 45-MINUTE WORKOUT ◯

## REFLECTION OF THE DAY

**Physical Health** _____

**Mental Health** _____

**The Things that Made You Feel Good Today** _____

## DIET STRATEGY

| Breakfast | _____ |
| Lunch | _____ |
| Dinner | _____ |
| Snacks | _____ |

## NOTES

## DAILY READING

BOOK TITEL _____
AUTHOR _____
PAGES _____

## WORKOUT PLAN

WORKOUT PLAN 1    WORKOUT PLAN 2

# 75 Day Soft Challenge

Date: _____  **S M T W T F S**

## DAY 26

- FOLLOW YOUR DIET ◯
- TAKE A PROGRESS PHOTO ◯
- DRINK 3L WATER EVERYDAY ◯
- READ 10 PAGES DAILY ◯
- DAILY 45-MINUTE WORKOUT ◯

## REFLECTION OF THE DAY

**Physical Health**
_____
_____
_____

**Mental Health**
_____
_____
_____

**The Things that Made You Feel Good Today**
_____
_____
_____

## DIET STRATEGY

Breakfast
_____
_____

Lunch
_____
_____

Dinner
_____
_____

Snacks
_____
_____

## NOTES

## DAILY READING

BOOK TITEL _____
AUTHOR _____
PAGES _____

## WORKOUT PLAN

WORKOUT PLAN 1      WORKOUT PLAN 2

# 75 Day Soft Challenge

Date: _____  S  M  T  W  T  F  S

## DAY
## 27

- FOLLOW YOUR DIET ⭘
- TAKE A PROGRESS PHOTO ⭘
- DRINK 3L WATER EVERYDAY ⭘
- READ 10 PAGES DAILY ⭘
- DAILY 45-MINUTE WORKOUT ⭘

## REFLECTION OF THE DAY

| Physical Health | |
| Mental Health | |
| The Things that Made You Feel Good Today | |

## DIET STRATEGY

| Breakfast | |
| Lunch | |
| Dinner | |
| Snacks | |

## NOTES

## DAILY READING

BOOK TITEL
AUTHOR
PAGES

## WORKOUT PLAN

| WORKOUT PLAN 1 | WORKOUT PLAN 2 |

# 75 Day Soft Challenge

Date: _____    S   M   T   W   T   F   S

## DAY 28

- FOLLOW YOUR DIET ◯
- TAKE A PROGRESS PHOTO ◯
- DRINK 3L WATER EVERYDAY ◯
- READ 10 PAGES DAILY ◯
- DAILY 45-MINUTE WORKOUT ◯

## REFLECTION OF THE DAY

**Physical Health** _____

**Mental Health** _____

**The Things that Made You Feel Good Today** _____

## DIET STRATEGY

Breakfast _____

Lunch _____

Dinner _____

Snacks _____

## NOTES

## DAILY READING

BOOK TITEL _____

AUTHOR _____

PAGES _____

## WORKOUT PLAN

| WORKOUT PLAN 1 | WORKOUT PLAN 2 |
| --- | --- |
| | |

# 75 Days Soft Challenges

## NOTES

# 75 Days Soft Challenges

## WEEKLY MEASURUMENTS

**Week 5**

| | |
|---|---|
| START DAY | _____ |
| START GOAL | _____ |
| FINISH DAY | _____ |
| FINISH GOAL | _____ |

| WEIGHT | ARM | CHEST | WAIST |
|---|---|---|---|
| | | | |

| BELLY | HIP | THIGH | CALF |
|---|---|---|---|
| | | | |

## WEEKLY MEAL PLANNING

| DAY | BREAKFAST | LUNCH | DINNER | SNACKS | TOTAL CAL |
|---|---|---|---|---|---|
| 1 | | | | | |
| 2 | | | | | |
| 3 | | | | | |
| 4 | | | | | |
| 5 | | | | | |
| 6 | | | | | |
| 7 | | | | | |

# 75 Days Soft Challenges

## GROCERY SHOPPING LIST

## NOTES

# 75 Day Soft Challenge

**Date:** _____     S  M  T  W  T  F  S

## DAY
## 29

- FOLLOW YOUR DIET ○
- TAKE A PROGRESS PHOTO ○
- DRINK 3L WATER EVERYDAY ○
- READ 10 PAGES DAILY ○
- DAILY 45-MINUTE WORKOUT ○

## REFLECTION OF THE DAY

| **Physical Health** | |
| **Mental Health** | |
| The Things that Made You Feel Good Today | |

## DIET STRATEGY

| Breakfast | |
| Lunch | |
| Dinner | |
| Snacks | |

## NOTES

## DAILY READING

BOOK TITEL

AUTHOR

PAGES

## WORKOUT PLAN

WORKOUT PLAN 1     WORKOUT PLAN 2

# 75 Day Soft Challenge

**Date:** _____  S  M  T  W  T  F  S

## DAY
### 30

- FOLLOW YOUR DIET ○
- TAKE A PROGRESS PHOTO ○
- DRINK 3L WATER EVERYDAY ○
- READ 10 PAGES DAILY ○
- DAILY 45-MINUTE WORKOUT ○

## REFLECTION OF THE DAY

**Physical Health** _____

**Mental Health** _____

**The Things that Made You Feel Good Today** _____

## DIET STRATEGY

**Breakfast** _____

**Lunch** _____

**Dinner** _____

**Snacks** _____

## NOTES

## DAILY READING

BOOK TITEL _____

AUTHOR _____

PAGES _____

## WORKOUT PLAN

WORKOUT PLAN 1

WORKOUT PLAN 2

# 75 Day Soft Challenge

Date: _____  **S  M  T  W  T  F  S**

## DAY 31

- FOLLOW YOUR DIET ○
- TAKE A PROGRESS PHOTO ○
- DRINK 3L WATER EVERYDAY ○
- READ 10 PAGES DAILY ○
- DAILY 45-MINUTE WORKOUT ○

## REFLECTION OF THE DAY

| Physical Health | |
| Mental Health | |
| The Things that Made You Feel Good Today | |

## DIET STRATEGY

| Breakfast | |
| Lunch | |
| Dinner | |
| Snacks | |

## NOTES

## DAILY READING

BOOK TITEL
AUTHOR
PAGES

## WORKOUT PLAN

| WORKOUT PLAN 1 | WORKOUT PLAN 2 |

# 75 Day Soft Challenge

**Date:** _____    S  M  T  W  T  F  S

## DAY
## 32

- FOLLOW YOUR DIET ○
- TAKE A PROGRESS PHOTO ○
- DRINK 3L WATER EVERYDAY ○
- READ 10 PAGES DAILY ○
- DAILY 45-MINUTE WORKOUT ○

## REFLECTION OF THE DAY

**Physical Health**

**Mental Health**

**The Things that Made You Feel Good Today**

## DIET STRATEGY

Breakfast

Lunch

Dinner

Snacks

## NOTES

## DAILY READING

BOOK TITEL

AUTHOR

PAGES

## WORKOUT PLAN

WORKOUT PLAN 1    WORKOUT PLAN 2

# 75 Day Soft Challenge

**Date:** _____

S  M  T  W  T  F  S

## DAY
## 33

- FOLLOW YOUR DIET ○
- TAKE A PROGRESS PHOTO ○
- DRINK 3L WATER EVERYDAY ○
- READ 10 PAGES DAILY ○
- DAILY 45-MINUTE WORKOUT ○

## REFLECTION OF THE DAY

**Physical Health** _____

**Mental Health** _____

**The Things that Made You Feel Good Today** _____

## DIET STRATEGY

Breakfast _____

Lunch _____

Dinner _____

Snacks _____

## NOTES

## DAILY  READING

BOOK TITEL _____

AUTHOR _____

PAGES _____

## WORKOUT  PLAN

WORKOUT PLAN 1

WORKOUT PLAN 2

# 75 Day Soft Challenge

Date: _____   S  M  T  W  T  F  S

## DAY 34

- FOLLOW YOUR DIET ◯
- TAKE A PROGRESS PHOTO ◯
- DRINK 3L WATER EVERYDAY ◯
- READ 10 PAGES DAILY ◯
- DAILY 45-MINUTE WORKOUT ◯

## REFLECTION OF THE DAY

**Physical Health** _____

**Mental Health** _____

**The Things that Made You Feel Good Today** _____

## DIET STRATEGY

Breakfast _____

Lunch _____

Dinner _____

Snacks _____

## NOTES

## DAILY READING

BOOK TITEL _____

AUTHOR _____

PAGES _____

## WORKOUT PLAN

WORKOUT PLAN 1

WORKOUT PLAN 2

# 75 Day Soft Challenge

Date: _____  S M T W T F S

## DAY 35

- FOLLOW YOUR DIET ⬜
- TAKE A PROGRESS PHOTO ⬜
- DRINK 3L WATER EVERYDAY ⬜
- READ 10 PAGES DAILY ⬜
- DAILY 45-MINUTE WORKOUT ⬜

## REFLECTION OF THE DAY

**Physical Health** _____

**Mental Health** _____

**The Things that Made You Feel Good Today** _____

## DIET STRATEGY

Breakfast _____

Lunch _____

Dinner _____

Snacks _____

## NOTES

## DAILY READING

BOOK TITEL _____

AUTHOR _____

PAGES _____

## WORKOUT PLAN

WORKOUT PLAN 1

WORKOUT PLAN 2

# 75 Days Soft Challenges

## NOTES

# 75 Days Soft Challenges

## WEEKLY MEASURUMENTS

### Week 6

| | |
|---|---|
| START DAY | _____ |
| START GOAL | _____ |
| FINISH DAY | _____ |
| FINISH GOAL | _____ |

| WEIGHT | ARM | CHEST | WAIST |
|---|---|---|---|
| | | | |

| BELLY | HIP | THIGH | CALF |
|---|---|---|---|
| | | | |

## WEEKLY MEAL PLANNING

| DAY | BREAKFAST | LUNCH | DINNER | SNACKS | TOTAL CAL |
|---|---|---|---|---|---|
| 1 | | | | | |
| 2 | | | | | |
| 3 | | | | | |
| 4 | | | | | |
| 5 | | | | | |
| 6 | | | | | |
| 7 | | | | | |

# 75 Days Soft Challenges

## GROCERY SHOPPING LIST

- ○ _____
- ○ _____
- ○ _____
- ○ _____
- ○ _____
- ○ _____
- ○ _____

- ○ _____
- ○ _____
- ○ _____
- ○ _____
- ○ _____
- ○ _____
- ○ _____

- ○ _____
- ○ _____
- ○ _____
- ○ _____
- ○ _____
- ○ _____
- ○ _____

## NOTES

_____

_____

_____

_____

_____

_____

_____

_____

_____

_____

_____

_____

# 75 Day Soft Challenge

**Date:** _____  S  M  T  W  T  F  S

## DAY 36

- FOLLOW YOUR DIET ○
- TAKE A PROGRESS PHOTO ○
- DRINK 3L WATER EVERYDAY ○
- READ 10 PAGES DAILY ○
- DAILY 45-MINUTE WORKOUT ○

## REFLECTION OF THE DAY

| | |
|---|---|
| **Physical Health** | _____ |
| **Mental Health** | _____ |
| The Things that Made You Feel Good Today | _____ |

## DIET STRATEGY

| | |
|---|---|
| Breakfast | _____ |
| Lunch | _____ |
| Dinner | _____ |
| Snacks | _____ |

## NOTES

## DAILY READING

BOOK TITEL _____
AUTHOR _____
PAGES _____

## WORKOUT PLAN

WORKOUT PLAN 1     WORKOUT PLAN 2

# 75 Day Soft Challenge

Date: _____  **S M T W T F S**

## DAY 37

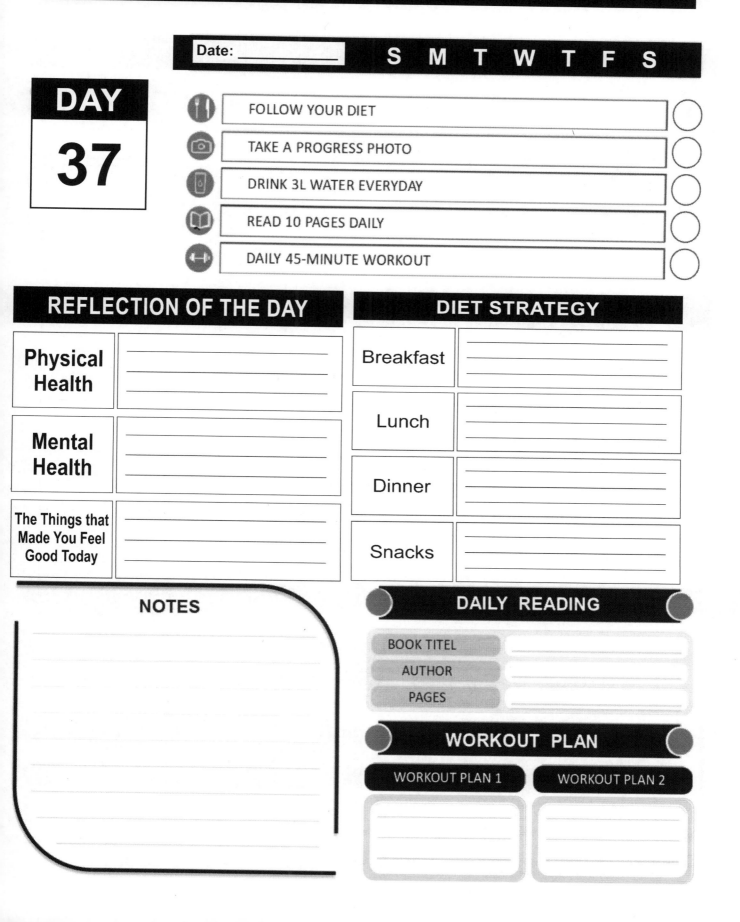

- FOLLOW YOUR DIET
- TAKE A PROGRESS PHOTO
- DRINK 3L WATER EVERYDAY
- READ 10 PAGES DAILY
- DAILY 45-MINUTE WORKOUT

## REFLECTION OF THE DAY

**Physical Health**

**Mental Health**

**The Things that Made You Feel Good Today**

## DIET STRATEGY

Breakfast

Lunch

Dinner

Snacks

## NOTES

## DAILY READING

BOOK TITEL

AUTHOR

PAGES

## WORKOUT PLAN

WORKOUT PLAN 1

WORKOUT PLAN 2

# 75 Day Soft Challenge

Date: _____  S  M  T  W  T  F  S

## DAY 38

- FOLLOW YOUR DIET ○
- TAKE A PROGRESS PHOTO ○
- DRINK 3L WATER EVERYDAY ○
- READ 10 PAGES DAILY ○
- DAILY 45-MINUTE WORKOUT ○

## REFLECTION OF THE DAY

**Physical Health** _____

**Mental Health** _____

**The Things that Made You Feel Good Today** _____

## DIET STRATEGY

Breakfast _____

Lunch _____

Dinner _____

Snacks _____

## NOTES

## DAILY READING

BOOK TITEL _____
AUTHOR _____
PAGES _____

## WORKOUT PLAN

| WORKOUT PLAN 1 | WORKOUT PLAN 2 |
| --- | --- |
| | |

# 75 Day Soft Challenge

Date: _____     **S M T W T F S**

**DAY**
**39**

- FOLLOW YOUR DIET
- TAKE A PROGRESS PHOTO
- DRINK 3L WATER EVERYDAY
- READ 10 PAGES DAILY
- DAILY 45-MINUTE WORKOUT

## REFLECTION OF THE DAY

| | |
|---|---|
| **Physical Health** | |
| **Mental Health** | |
| **The Things that Made You Feel Good Today** | |

## DIET STRATEGY

| | |
|---|---|
| Breakfast | |
| Lunch | |
| Dinner | |
| Snacks | |

## NOTES

## DAILY READING

| | |
|---|---|
| BOOK TITEL | |
| AUTHOR | |
| PAGES | |

## WORKOUT PLAN

| WORKOUT PLAN 1 | WORKOUT PLAN 2 |
|---|---|
| | |

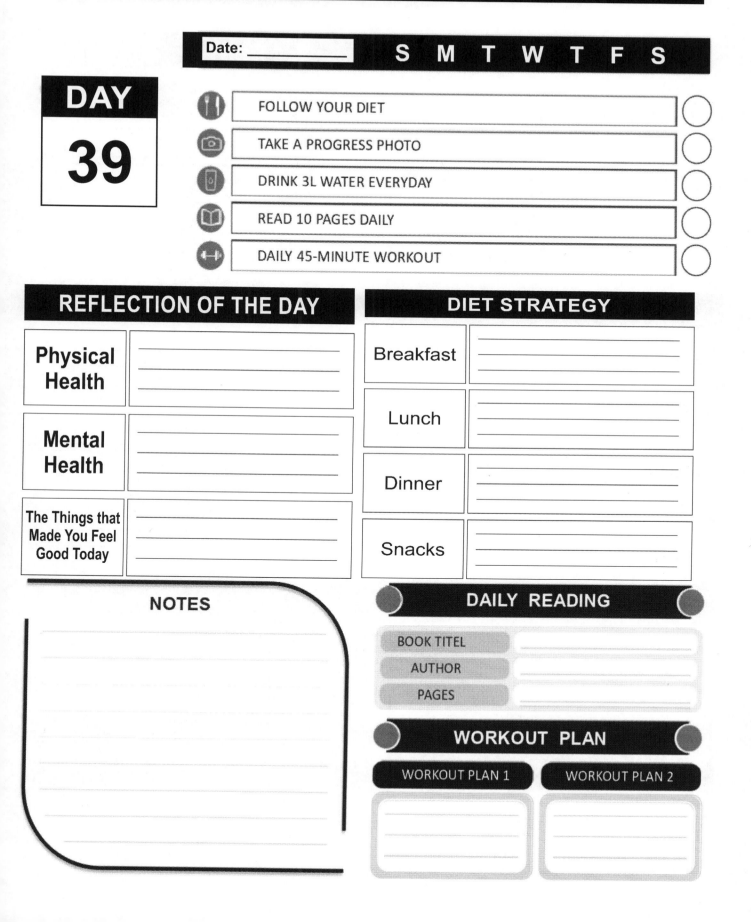

# 75 Day Soft Challenge

**Date:** _____    S M T W T F S

## DAY 40

- FOLLOW YOUR DIET ◯
- TAKE A PROGRESS PHOTO ◯
- DRINK 3L WATER EVERYDAY ◯
- READ 10 PAGES DAILY ◯
- DAILY 45-MINUTE WORKOUT ◯

## REFLECTION OF THE DAY

**Physical Health** _____

**Mental Health** _____

**The Things that Made You Feel Good Today** _____

## DIET STRATEGY

**Breakfast** _____

**Lunch** _____

**Dinner** _____

**Snacks** _____

## NOTES

## DAILY READING

BOOK TITEL _____
AUTHOR _____
PAGES _____

## WORKOUT PLAN

WORKOUT PLAN 1
WORKOUT PLAN 2

# 75 Day Soft Challenge

**Date:** _____  **S  M  T  W  T  F  S**

## DAY
## 41

- FOLLOW YOUR DIET ○
- TAKE A PROGRESS PHOTO ○
- DRINK 3L WATER EVERYDAY ○
- READ 10 PAGES DAILY ○
- DAILY 45-MINUTE WORKOUT ○

## REFLECTION OF THE DAY

**Physical Health** _____

**Mental Health** _____

**The Things that Made You Feel Good Today** _____

## DIET STRATEGY

Breakfast _____

Lunch _____

Dinner _____

Snacks _____

## NOTES

## DAILY READING

BOOK TITEL _____

AUTHOR _____

PAGES _____

## WORKOUT PLAN

WORKOUT PLAN 1 | WORKOUT PLAN 2

# 75 Day Soft Challenge

Date: _____  S  M  T  W  T  F  S

## DAY
## 42

- FOLLOW YOUR DIET ○
- TAKE A PROGRESS PHOTO ○
- DRINK 3L WATER EVERYDAY ○
- READ 10 PAGES DAILY ○
- DAILY 45-MINUTE WORKOUT ○

## REFLECTION OF THE DAY

**Physical Health** | _____

**Mental Health** | _____

**The Things that Made You Feel Good Today** | _____

## DIET STRATEGY

Breakfast | _____

Lunch | _____

Dinner | _____

Snacks | _____

## NOTES

## DAILY READING

BOOK TITEL | _____
AUTHOR | _____
PAGES | _____

## WORKOUT PLAN

WORKOUT PLAN 1 | WORKOUT PLAN 2

# 75 Days Soft Challenges

## NOTES

# 75 Days Soft Challenges

## WEEKLY MEASURUMENTS

**Week 7**

| START DAY | |
|-----------|--|
| START GOAL | |
| FINISH DAY | |
| FINISH GOAL | |

| WEIGHT | ARM | CHEST | WAIST |
|--------|-----|-------|-------|
| | | | |

| BELLY | HIP | THIGH | CALF |
|-------|-----|-------|------|
| | | | |

## WEEKLY MEAL PLANNING

| DAY | BREAKFAST | LUNCH | DINNER | SNACKS | TOTAL CAL |
|-----|-----------|-------|--------|--------|-----------|
| 1 | | | | | |
| 2 | | | | | |
| 3 | | | | | |
| 4 | | | | | |
| 5 | | | | | |
| 6 | | | | | |
| 7 | | | | | |

# 75 Days Soft Challenges

## GROCERY SHOPPING LIST

- ⬭ _____
- ⬭ _____
- ⬭ _____
- ⬭ _____
- ⬭ _____
- ⬭ _____
- ⬭ _____

- ⬭ _____
- ⬭ _____
- ⬭ _____
- ⬭ _____
- ⬭ _____
- ⬭ _____
- ⬭ _____

- ⬭ _____
- ⬭ _____
- ⬭ _____
- ⬭ _____
- ⬭ _____
- ⬭ _____
- ⬭ _____

## NOTES

_____

_____

_____

_____

_____

_____

_____

_____

_____

_____

_____

_____

# 75 Day Soft Challenge

**Date:** _____  **S  M  T  W  T  F  S**

## DAY
## 43

- FOLLOW YOUR DIET ○
- TAKE A PROGRESS PHOTO ○
- DRINK 3L WATER EVERYDAY ○
- READ 10 PAGES DAILY ○
- DAILY 45-MINUTE WORKOUT ○

## REFLECTION OF THE DAY

| | |
|---|---|
| **Physical Health** | _____ |
| **Mental Health** | _____ |
| **The Things that Made You Feel Good Today** | _____ |

## DIET STRATEGY

| | |
|---|---|
| Breakfast | _____ |
| Lunch | _____ |
| Dinner | _____ |
| Snacks | _____ |

## NOTES

## DAILY READING

| BOOK TITEL | _____ |
|---|---|
| AUTHOR | _____ |
| PAGES | _____ |

## WORKOUT PLAN

| WORKOUT PLAN 1 | WORKOUT PLAN 2 |
|---|---|
| | |

# 75 Day Soft Challenge

Date: _____  **S  M  T  W  T  F  S**

## DAY
## 44

- FOLLOW YOUR DIET ○
- TAKE A PROGRESS PHOTO ○
- DRINK 3L WATER EVERYDAY ○
- READ 10 PAGES DAILY ○
- DAILY 45-MINUTE WORKOUT ○

## REFLECTION OF THE DAY

| | |
|---|---|
| **Physical Health** | |
| **Mental Health** | |
| **The Things that Made You Feel Good Today** | |

## DIET STRATEGY

| | |
|---|---|
| Breakfast | |
| Lunch | |
| Dinner | |
| Snacks | |

## NOTES

## DAILY READING

BOOK TITEL
AUTHOR
PAGES

## WORKOUT PLAN

WORKOUT PLAN 1

WORKOUT PLAN 2

# 75 Day Soft Challenge

**Date:** _____     **S  M  T  W  T  F  S**

## DAY
## 45

- FOLLOW YOUR DIET
- TAKE A PROGRESS PHOTO
- DRINK 3L WATER EVERYDAY
- READ 10 PAGES DAILY
- DAILY 45-MINUTE WORKOUT

## REFLECTION OF THE DAY

**Physical Health** _____

**Mental Health** _____

**The Things that Made You Feel Good Today** _____

## DIET STRATEGY

Breakfast _____

Lunch _____

Dinner _____

Snacks _____

## NOTES

## DAILY READING

BOOK TITEL _____
AUTHOR _____
PAGES _____

## WORKOUT PLAN

WORKOUT PLAN 1     WORKOUT PLAN 2

# 75 Day Soft Challenge

Date: _____  **S M T W T F S**

## DAY 46

- FOLLOW YOUR DIET ⭕
- TAKE A PROGRESS PHOTO ⭕
- DRINK 3L WATER EVERYDAY ⭕
- READ 10 PAGES DAILY ⭕
- DAILY 45-MINUTE WORKOUT ⭕

## REFLECTION OF THE DAY

| Physical Health | _____ |
| Mental Health | _____ |
| The Things that Made You Feel Good Today | _____ |

## DIET STRATEGY

| Breakfast | _____ |
| Lunch | _____ |
| Dinner | _____ |
| Snacks | _____ |

## NOTES

## DAILY READING

| BOOK TITEL | _____ |
| AUTHOR | _____ |
| PAGES | _____ |

## WORKOUT PLAN

| WORKOUT PLAN 1 | WORKOUT PLAN 2 |

# 75 Day Soft Challenge

Date: _____    S  M  T  W  T  F  S

**DAY 47**

- FOLLOW YOUR DIET ⭕
- TAKE A PROGRESS PHOTO ⭕
- DRINK 3L WATER EVERYDAY ⭕
- READ 10 PAGES DAILY ⭕
- DAILY 45-MINUTE WORKOUT ⭕

## REFLECTION OF THE DAY

**Physical Health**
_____
_____
_____

**Mental Health**
_____
_____
_____

**The Things that Made You Feel Good Today**
_____
_____
_____

## DIET STRATEGY

**Breakfast**
_____
_____

**Lunch**
_____
_____

**Dinner**
_____
_____

**Snacks**
_____
_____

## NOTES

_____
_____
_____
_____
_____
_____

## DAILY READING

| BOOK TITEL | |
| AUTHOR | |
| PAGES | |

## WORKOUT PLAN

| WORKOUT PLAN 1 | WORKOUT PLAN 2 |
| --- | --- |
| | |

# 75 Day Soft Challenge

Date: _____  S M T W T F S

## DAY 48

- FOLLOW YOUR DIET ○
- TAKE A PROGRESS PHOTO ○
- DRINK 3L WATER EVERYDAY ○
- READ 10 PAGES DAILY ○
- DAILY 45-MINUTE WORKOUT ○

## REFLECTION OF THE DAY

| Physical Health | _____ |
| Mental Health | _____ |
| The Things that Made You Feel Good Today | _____ |

## DIET STRATEGY

| Breakfast | _____ |
| Lunch | _____ |
| Dinner | _____ |
| Snacks | _____ |

## NOTES

## DAILY READING

| BOOK TITEL | |
| AUTHOR | |
| PAGES | |

## WORKOUT PLAN

| WORKOUT PLAN 1 | WORKOUT PLAN 2 |

# 75 Day Soft Challenge

**Date:** _____  S M T W T F S

## DAY 49

- FOLLOW YOUR DIET ○
- TAKE A PROGRESS PHOTO ○
- DRINK 3L WATER EVERYDAY ○
- READ 10 PAGES DAILY ○
- DAILY 45-MINUTE WORKOUT ○

## REFLECTION OF THE DAY

**Physical Health**
_____
_____

**Mental Health**
_____
_____

**The Things that Made You Feel Good Today**
_____
_____

## DIET STRATEGY

**Breakfast**
_____
_____

**Lunch**
_____
_____

**Dinner**
_____
_____

**Snacks**
_____
_____

## NOTES

## DAILY READING

| BOOK TITEL | |
| AUTHOR | |
| PAGES | |

## WORKOUT PLAN

| WORKOUT PLAN 1 | WORKOUT PLAN 2 |
| --- | --- |
| | |

# 75 Days Soft Challenges

## NOTES

_____
_____
_____
_____
_____
_____
_____
_____
_____
_____
_____
_____
_____
_____
_____
_____
_____
_____
_____
_____
_____

# 75 Days Soft Challenges

## WEEKLY MEASURUMENTS

| Week | | |
|------|--|--|
| **8** | START DAY | |
| | START GOAL | |
| | FINISH DAY | |
| | FINISH GOAL | |

| WEIGHT | ARM | CHEST | WAIST |
|--------|-----|-------|-------|
| | | | |

| BELLY | HIP | THIGH | CALF |
|-------|-----|-------|------|
| | | | |

## WEEKLY MEAL PLANNING

| DAY | BREAKFAST | LUNCH | DINNER | SNACKS | TOTAL CAL |
|-----|-----------|-------|--------|--------|-----------|
| 1 | | | | | |
| 2 | | | | | |
| 3 | | | | | |
| 4 | | | | | |
| 5 | | | | | |
| 6 | | | | | |
| 7 | | | | | |

# 75 Days Soft Challenges

## GROCERY SHOPPING LIST

- ◯ _____
- ◯ _____
- ◯ _____
- ◯ _____
- ◯ _____
- ◯ _____
- ◯ _____

- ◯ _____
- ◯ _____
- ◯ _____
- ◯ _____
- ◯ _____
- ◯ _____
- ◯ _____

- ◯ _____
- ◯ _____
- ◯ _____
- ◯ _____
- ◯ _____
- ◯ _____
- ◯ _____

## NOTES

_____
_____
_____
_____
_____
_____
_____
_____
_____
_____
_____
_____
_____

# 75 Day Soft Challenge

**Date:** _____     S  M  T  W  T  F  S

## DAY
## 50

- FOLLOW YOUR DIET ⭕
- TAKE A PROGRESS PHOTO ⭕
- DRINK 3L WATER EVERYDAY ⭕
- READ 10 PAGES DAILY ⭕
- DAILY 45-MINUTE WORKOUT ⭕

## REFLECTION OF THE DAY

**Physical Health** _____

**Mental Health** _____

**The Things that Made You Feel Good Today** _____

## DIET STRATEGY

Breakfast _____

Lunch _____

Dinner _____

Snacks _____

## NOTES

## DAILY READING

BOOK TITEL _____

AUTHOR _____

PAGES _____

## WORKOUT PLAN

WORKOUT PLAN 1          WORKOUT PLAN 2

# 75 Day Soft Challenge

Date: _____    S  M  T  W  T  F  S

## DAY
## 51

- FOLLOW YOUR DIET ○
- TAKE A PROGRESS PHOTO ○
- DRINK 3L WATER EVERYDAY ○
- READ 10 PAGES DAILY ○
- DAILY 45-MINUTE WORKOUT ○

## REFLECTION OF THE DAY

| Physical Health | _____ |
| Mental Health | _____ |
| The Things that Made You Feel Good Today | _____ |

## DIET STRATEGY

| Breakfast | _____ |
| Lunch | _____ |
| Dinner | _____ |
| Snacks | _____ |

## NOTES

## DAILY READING

BOOK TITEL _____
AUTHOR _____
PAGES _____

## WORKOUT PLAN

WORKOUT PLAN 1     WORKOUT PLAN 2

# 75 Day Soft Challenge

Date: _____          **S  M  T  W  T  F  S**

**DAY**
**52**

- FOLLOW YOUR DIET ○
- TAKE A PROGRESS PHOTO ○
- DRINK 3L WATER EVERYDAY ○
- READ 10 PAGES DAILY ○
- DAILY 45-MINUTE WORKOUT ○

## REFLECTION OF THE DAY

| **Physical Health** | _____ |
| **Mental Health** | _____ |
| The Things that Made You Feel Good Today | _____ |

## DIET STRATEGY

| Breakfast | _____ |
| Lunch | _____ |
| Dinner | _____ |
| Snacks | _____ |

## NOTES

## DAILY READING

| BOOK TITEL | _____ |
| AUTHOR | _____ |
| PAGES | _____ |

## WORKOUT PLAN

| WORKOUT PLAN 1 | WORKOUT PLAN 2 |

# 75 Day Soft Challenge

Date: _____  S M T W T F S

## DAY 53

- FOLLOW YOUR DIET ○
- TAKE A PROGRESS PHOTO ○
- DRINK 3L WATER EVERYDAY ○
- READ 10 PAGES DAILY ○
- DAILY 45-MINUTE WORKOUT ○

## REFLECTION OF THE DAY

**Physical Health**
_____
_____
_____

**Mental Health**
_____
_____
_____

**The Things that Made You Feel Good Today**
_____
_____
_____

## DIET STRATEGY

Breakfast
_____
_____

Lunch
_____
_____

Dinner
_____
_____

Snacks
_____
_____

## NOTES

## DAILY READING

BOOK TITEL _____
AUTHOR _____
PAGES _____

## WORKOUT PLAN

WORKOUT PLAN 1  WORKOUT PLAN 2

# 75 Day Soft Challenge

**Date:** _____  S  M  T  W  T  F  S

## DAY
## 54

- FOLLOW YOUR DIET ○
- TAKE A PROGRESS PHOTO ○
- DRINK 3L WATER EVERYDAY ○
- READ 10 PAGES DAILY ○
- DAILY 45-MINUTE WORKOUT ○

## REFLECTION OF THE DAY

| **Physical Health** | _____ |
| **Mental Health** | _____ |
| **The Things that Made You Feel Good Today** | _____ |

## DIET STRATEGY

| Breakfast | _____ |
| Lunch | _____ |
| Dinner | _____ |
| Snacks | _____ |

## NOTES

## DAILY READING

| BOOK TITEL | |
| AUTHOR | |
| PAGES | |

## WORKOUT PLAN

| WORKOUT PLAN 1 | WORKOUT PLAN 2 |

# 75 Day Soft Challenge

**Date:** _____     S  M  T  W  T  F  S

## DAY
### 55

- FOLLOW YOUR DIET ○
- TAKE A PROGRESS PHOTO ○
- DRINK 3L WATER EVERYDAY ○
- READ 10 PAGES DAILY ○
- DAILY 45-MINUTE WORKOUT ○

## REFLECTION OF THE DAY

**Physical Health**

**Mental Health**

**The Things that Made You Feel Good Today**

## DIET STRATEGY

Breakfast

Lunch

Dinner

Snacks

## NOTES

## DAILY READING

BOOK TITEL

AUTHOR

PAGES

## WORKOUT PLAN

WORKOUT PLAN 1 | WORKOUT PLAN 2

# 75 Day Soft Challenge

**Date:** _____    **S  M  T  W  T  F  S**

## DAY 56

- FOLLOW YOUR DIET ○
- TAKE A PROGRESS PHOTO ○
- DRINK 3L WATER EVERYDAY ○
- READ 10 PAGES DAILY ○
- DAILY 45-MINUTE WORKOUT ○

## REFLECTION OF THE DAY

**Physical Health** _____

**Mental Health** _____

**The Things that Made You Feel Good Today** _____

## DIET STRATEGY

**Breakfast** _____

**Lunch** _____

**Dinner** _____

**Snacks** _____

## NOTES

## DAILY READING

BOOK TITEL _____
AUTHOR _____
PAGES _____

## WORKOUT PLAN

WORKOUT PLAN 1

WORKOUT PLAN 2

# 75 Days Soft Challenges

## NOTES

# 75 Days Soft Challenges

## WEEKLY MEASURUMENTS

**Week 9**

| | |
|---|---|
| START DAY | _____ |
| START GOAL | _____ |
| FINISH DAY | _____ |
| FINISH GOAL | _____ |

| WEIGHT | ARM | CHEST | WAIST |
|---|---|---|---|
| | | | |

| BELLY | HIP | THIGH | CALF |
|---|---|---|---|
| | | | |

## WEEKLY MEAL PLANNING

| DAY | BREAKFAST | LUNCH | DINNER | SNACKS | TOTAL CAL |
|---|---|---|---|---|---|
| 1 | | | | | |
| 2 | | | | | |
| 3 | | | | | |
| 4 | | | | | |
| 5 | | | | | |
| 6 | | | | | |
| 7 | | | | | |

# 75 Days Soft Challenges

## GROCERY SHOPPING LIST

○ _____    ○ _____    ○ _____
○ _____    ○ _____    ○ _____
○ _____    ○ _____    ○ _____
○ _____    ○ _____    ○ _____
○ _____    ○ _____    ○ _____
○ _____    ○ _____    ○ _____
○ _____    ○ _____    ○ _____

## NOTES

_____

_____

_____

_____

_____

_____

_____

_____

_____

_____

_____

_____

_____

# 75 Day Soft Challenge

Date: _____    S  M  T  W  T  F  S

## DAY
## 57

- FOLLOW YOUR DIET ⭘
- TAKE A PROGRESS PHOTO ⭘
- DRINK 3L WATER EVERYDAY ⭘
- READ 10 PAGES DAILY ⭘
- DAILY 45-MINUTE WORKOUT ⭘

## REFLECTION OF THE DAY

| Physical Health | _____ |
| Mental Health | _____ |
| The Things that Made You Feel Good Today | _____ |

## DIET STRATEGY

| Breakfast | _____ |
| Lunch | _____ |
| Dinner | _____ |
| Snacks | _____ |

## NOTES

## DAILY READING

BOOK TITEL _____
AUTHOR _____
PAGES _____

## WORKOUT PLAN

WORKOUT PLAN 1          WORKOUT PLAN 2

# 75 Day Soft Challenge

Date: _____   **S  M  T  W  T  F  S**

## DAY 58

- FOLLOW YOUR DIET ◯
- TAKE A PROGRESS PHOTO ◯
- DRINK 3L WATER EVERYDAY ◯
- READ 10 PAGES DAILY ◯
- DAILY 45-MINUTE WORKOUT ◯

## REFLECTION OF THE DAY

**Physical Health** _____

**Mental Health** _____

**The Things that Made You Feel Good Today** _____

## DIET STRATEGY

**Breakfast** _____

**Lunch** _____

**Dinner** _____

**Snacks** _____

## NOTES

## DAILY READING

BOOK TITEL _____
AUTHOR _____
PAGES _____

## WORKOUT PLAN

WORKOUT PLAN 1   WORKOUT PLAN 2

# 75 Day Soft Challenge

Date: _____    S  M  T  W  T  F  S

## DAY
## 59

- FOLLOW YOUR DIET ○
- TAKE A PROGRESS PHOTO ○
- DRINK 3L WATER EVERYDAY ○
- READ 10 PAGES DAILY ○
- DAILY 45-MINUTE WORKOUT ○

## REFLECTION OF THE DAY

**Physical Health**
_____
_____
_____

**Mental Health**
_____
_____
_____

**The Things that Made You Feel Good Today**
_____
_____
_____

## DIET STRATEGY

Breakfast
_____
_____
_____

Lunch
_____
_____
_____

Dinner
_____
_____
_____

Snacks
_____
_____
_____

## NOTES

## DAILY READING

BOOK TITEL _____
AUTHOR _____
PAGES _____

## WORKOUT PLAN

WORKOUT PLAN 1          WORKOUT PLAN 2

# 75 Day Soft Challenge

**Date:** _____     S  M  T  W  T  F  S

## DAY 60

- FOLLOW YOUR DIET ◯
- TAKE A PROGRESS PHOTO ◯
- DRINK 3L WATER EVERYDAY ◯
- READ 10 PAGES DAILY ◯
- DAILY 45-MINUTE WORKOUT ◯

## REFLECTION OF THE DAY

**Physical Health** _____

**Mental Health** _____

**The Things that Made You Feel Good Today** _____

## DIET STRATEGY

Breakfast _____

Lunch _____

Dinner _____

Snacks _____

## NOTES

_____

## DAILY READING

BOOK TITEL _____
AUTHOR _____
PAGES _____

## WORKOUT PLAN

WORKOUT PLAN 1

WORKOUT PLAN 2

# 75 Day Soft Challenge

Date: _____  S M T W T F S

## DAY 61

- FOLLOW YOUR DIET ○
- TAKE A PROGRESS PHOTO ○
- DRINK 3L WATER EVERYDAY ○
- READ 10 PAGES DAILY ○
- DAILY 45-MINUTE WORKOUT ○

## REFLECTION OF THE DAY

**Physical Health** _____

**Mental Health** _____

**The Things that Made You Feel Good Today** _____

## DIET STRATEGY

Breakfast _____

Lunch _____

Dinner _____

Snacks _____

## NOTES

## DAILY READING

BOOK TITEL _____
AUTHOR _____
PAGES _____

## WORKOUT PLAN

WORKOUT PLAN 1

WORKOUT PLAN 2

# 75 Day Soft Challenge

**Date:** _____   S  M  T  W  T  F  S

## DAY
## 62

- FOLLOW YOUR DIET ⭕
- TAKE A PROGRESS PHOTO ⭕
- DRINK 3L WATER EVERYDAY ⭕
- READ 10 PAGES DAILY ⭕
- DAILY 45-MINUTE WORKOUT ⭕

## REFLECTION OF THE DAY

| Physical Health | _____ |
| Mental Health | _____ |
| The Things that Made You Feel Good Today | _____ |

## DIET STRATEGY

| Breakfast | _____ |
| Lunch | _____ |
| Dinner | _____ |
| Snacks | _____ |

## NOTES

## DAILY READING

| BOOK TITEL | _____ |
| AUTHOR | _____ |
| PAGES | _____ |

## WORKOUT PLAN

| WORKOUT PLAN 1 | WORKOUT PLAN 2 |

# 75 Day Soft Challenge

**Date:** _____  S  M  T  W  T  F  S

## DAY
## 63

- FOLLOW YOUR DIET ○
- TAKE A PROGRESS PHOTO ○
- DRINK 3L WATER EVERYDAY ○
- READ 10 PAGES DAILY ○
- DAILY 45-MINUTE WORKOUT ○

## REFLECTION OF THE DAY

| Physical Health | _____ |
| Mental Health | _____ |
| The Things that Made You Feel Good Today | _____ |

## DIET STRATEGY

| Breakfast | _____ |
| Lunch | _____ |
| Dinner | _____ |
| Snacks | _____ |

## NOTES

## DAILY READING

| BOOK TITEL | _____ |
| AUTHOR | _____ |
| PAGES | _____ |

## WORKOUT PLAN

| WORKOUT PLAN 1 | WORKOUT PLAN 2 |

# 75 Days Soft Challenges

## NOTES

# 75 Days Soft Challenges

## WEEKLY MEASURUMENTS

**Week 10**

START DAY _____

START GOAL _____

FINISH DAY _____

FINISH GOAL _____

| WEIGHT | ARM | CHEST | WAIST |
|--------|-----|-------|-------|
|        |     |       |       |

| BELLY | HIP | THIGH | CALF |
|-------|-----|-------|------|
|       |     |       |      |

## WEEKLY MEAL PLANNING

| DAY | BREAKFAST | LUNCH | DINNER | SNACKS | TOTAL CAL |
|-----|-----------|-------|--------|--------|-----------|
| 1   |           |       |        |        |           |
| 2   |           |       |        |        |           |
| 3   |           |       |        |        |           |
| 4   |           |       |        |        |           |
| 5   |           |       |        |        |           |
| 6   |           |       |        |        |           |
| 7   |           |       |        |        |           |

# 75 Days Soft Challenges

## GROCERY SHOPPING LIST

- ○ _____
- ○ _____
- ○ _____
- ○ _____
- ○ _____
- ○ _____
- ○ _____

- ○ _____
- ○ _____
- ○ _____
- ○ _____
- ○ _____
- ○ _____
- ○ _____

- ○ _____
- ○ _____
- ○ _____
- ○ _____
- ○ _____
- ○ _____
- ○ _____

## NOTES

_____

_____

_____

_____

_____

_____

_____

_____

_____

_____

_____

_____

_____

# 75 Day Soft Challenge

Date: _____    S  M  T  W  T  F  S

## DAY 64

- FOLLOW YOUR DIET ◯
- TAKE A PROGRESS PHOTO ◯
- DRINK 3L WATER EVERYDAY ◯
- READ 10 PAGES DAILY ◯
- DAILY 45-MINUTE WORKOUT ◯

## REFLECTION OF THE DAY

**Physical Health** _____

**Mental Health** _____

**The Things that Made You Feel Good Today** _____

## DIET STRATEGY

Breakfast _____

Lunch _____

Dinner _____

Snacks _____

## NOTES

## DAILY READING

BOOK TITEL _____
AUTHOR _____
PAGES _____

## WORKOUT PLAN

WORKOUT PLAN 1

WORKOUT PLAN 2

# 75 Day Soft Challenge

**Date:** _____    S  M  T  W  T  F  S

**DAY 65**

- FOLLOW YOUR DIET
- TAKE A PROGRESS PHOTO
- DRINK 3L WATER EVERYDAY
- READ 10 PAGES DAILY
- DAILY 45-MINUTE WORKOUT

## REFLECTION OF THE DAY

**Physical Health**

**Mental Health**

**The Things that Made You Feel Good Today**

## DIET STRATEGY

Breakfast

Lunch

Dinner

Snacks

## NOTES

## DAILY READING

BOOK TITEL

AUTHOR

PAGES

## WORKOUT PLAN

WORKOUT PLAN 1     WORKOUT PLAN 2

# 75 Day Soft Challenge

**Date:** _____    S  M  T  W  T  F  S

## DAY
## 67

- FOLLOW YOUR DIET ○
- TAKE A PROGRESS PHOTO ○
- DRINK 3L WATER EVERYDAY ○
- READ 10 PAGES DAILY ○
- DAILY 45-MINUTE WORKOUT ○

## REFLECTION OF THE DAY

| | |
|---|---|
| **Physical Health** | _____ |
| **Mental Health** | _____ |
| The Things that Made You Feel Good Today | _____ |

## DIET STRATEGY

| | |
|---|---|
| Breakfast | _____ |
| Lunch | _____ |
| Dinner | _____ |
| Snacks | _____ |

## NOTES

## DAILY READING

| BOOK TITEL | |
|---|---|
| AUTHOR | |
| PAGES | |

## WORKOUT PLAN

| WORKOUT PLAN 1 | WORKOUT PLAN 2 |
|---|---|
| | |

# 75 Day Soft Challenge

**Date:** _____  S  M  T  W  T  F  S

## DAY
## 68

- FOLLOW YOUR DIET ○
- TAKE A PROGRESS PHOTO ○
- DRINK 3L WATER EVERYDAY ○
- READ 10 PAGES DAILY ○
- DAILY 45-MINUTE WORKOUT ○

## REFLECTION OF THE DAY

**Physical Health** _____

**Mental Health** _____

**The Things that Made You Feel Good Today** _____

## DIET STRATEGY

Breakfast _____

Lunch _____

Dinner _____

Snacks _____

## NOTES

## DAILY READING

BOOK TITEL _____
AUTHOR _____
PAGES _____

## WORKOUT PLAN

WORKOUT PLAN 1     WORKOUT PLAN 2

# 75 Day Soft Challenge

**Date:** _____    S  M  T  W  T  F  S

## DAY
## 69

- FOLLOW YOUR DIET ○
- TAKE A PROGRESS PHOTO ○
- DRINK 3L WATER EVERYDAY ○
- READ 10 PAGES DAILY ○
- DAILY 45-MINUTE WORKOUT ○

## REFLECTION OF THE DAY

| **Physical Health** | |
| **Mental Health** | |
| **The Things that Made You Feel Good Today** | |

## DIET STRATEGY

| Breakfast | |
| Lunch | |
| Dinner | |
| Snacks | |

## NOTES

## DAILY READING

| BOOK TITEL | |
| AUTHOR | |
| PAGES | |

## WORKOUT PLAN

| WORKOUT PLAN 1 | WORKOUT PLAN 2 |
| | |

# 75 Day Soft Challenge

Date: _____  **S M T W T F S**

## DAY 70

- FOLLOW YOUR DIET ⭘
- TAKE A PROGRESS PHOTO ⭘
- DRINK 3L WATER EVERYDAY ⭘
- READ 10 PAGES DAILY ⭘
- DAILY 45-MINUTE WORKOUT ⭘

## REFLECTION OF THE DAY

**Physical Health** _____

**Mental Health** _____

**The Things that Made You Feel Good Today** _____

## DIET STRATEGY

Breakfast _____

Lunch _____

Dinner _____

Snacks _____

## NOTES

## DAILY READING

BOOK TITEL _____
AUTHOR _____
PAGES _____

## WORKOUT PLAN

| WORKOUT PLAN 1 | WORKOUT PLAN 2 |
|---|---|
| | |

# 75 Day Soft Challenge

**Date:** _____     S  M  T  W  T  F  S

## DAY
## 71

- FOLLOW YOUR DIET ◯
- TAKE A PROGRESS PHOTO ◯
- DRINK 3L WATER EVERYDAY ◯
- READ 10 PAGES DAILY ◯
- DAILY 45-MINUTE WORKOUT ◯

## REFLECTION OF THE DAY

**Physical Health** _____

**Mental Health** _____

**The Things that Made You Feel Good Today** _____

## DIET STRATEGY

| Breakfast | _____ |
| Lunch | _____ |
| Dinner | _____ |
| Snacks | _____ |

## NOTES

## DAILY READING

| BOOK TITEL | |
| AUTHOR | |
| PAGES | |

## WORKOUT PLAN

| WORKOUT PLAN 1 | WORKOUT PLAN 2 |

# 75 Days Soft Challenges

## NOTES

# 75 Days Soft Challenges

## WEEKLY MEASURUMENTS

**Week 11**

| START DAY | _____ |
| START GOAL | _____ |
| FINISH DAY | _____ |
| FINISH GOAL | _____ |

| WEIGHT | ARM | CHEST | WAIST |
|--------|-----|-------|-------|
| | | | |

| BELLY | HIP | THIGH | CALF |
|-------|-----|-------|------|
| | | | |

## WEEKLY MEAL PLANNING

| DAY | BREAKFAST | LUNCH | DINNER | SNACKS | TOTAL CAL |
|-----|-----------|-------|--------|--------|-----------|
| 1 | | | | | |
| 2 | | | | | |
| 3 | | | | | |
| 4 | | | | | |
| 5 | | | | | |
| 6 | | | | | |
| 7 | | | | | |

# 75 Days Soft Challenges

## GROCERY SHOPPING LIST

- ◯ _____
- ◯ _____
- ◯ _____
- ◯ _____
- ◯ _____
- ◯ _____
- ◯ _____

- ◯ _____
- ◯ _____
- ◯ _____
- ◯ _____
- ◯ _____
- ◯ _____
- ◯ _____

- ◯ _____
- ◯ _____
- ◯ _____
- ◯ _____
- ◯ _____
- ◯ _____
- ◯ _____

## NOTES

_____

_____

_____

_____

_____

_____

_____

_____

_____

_____

_____

_____

# 75 Day Soft Challenge

Date: _____     **S  M  T  W  T  F  S**

## DAY
## 72

- FOLLOW YOUR DIET  ◯
- TAKE A PROGRESS PHOTO  ◯
- DRINK 3L WATER EVERYDAY  ◯
- READ 10 PAGES DAILY  ◯
- DAILY 45-MINUTE WORKOUT  ◯

## REFLECTION OF THE DAY

| **Physical Health** | _____ |
| **Mental Health** | _____ |
| The Things that Made You Feel Good Today | _____ |

## DIET STRATEGY

| Breakfast | _____ |
| Lunch | _____ |
| Dinner | _____ |
| Snacks | _____ |

## NOTES

## DAILY READING

| BOOK TITEL | _____ |
| AUTHOR | _____ |
| PAGES | _____ |

## WORKOUT PLAN

| WORKOUT PLAN 1 | WORKOUT PLAN 2 |

# 75 Day Soft Challenge

Date: _____     **S  M  T  W  T  F  S**

## DAY
## 73

- FOLLOW YOUR DIET ○
- TAKE A PROGRESS PHOTO ○
- DRINK 3L WATER EVERYDAY ○
- READ 10 PAGES DAILY ○
- DAILY 45-MINUTE WORKOUT ○

## REFLECTION OF THE DAY

**Physical Health** _____

**Mental Health** _____

**The Things that Made You Feel Good Today** _____

## DIET STRATEGY

Breakfast _____

Lunch _____

Dinner _____

Snacks _____

## NOTES

## DAILY READING

BOOK TITEL _____

AUTHOR _____

PAGES _____

## WORKOUT PLAN

WORKOUT PLAN 1          WORKOUT PLAN 2

# 75 Day Soft Challenge

Date: _____    S  M  T  W  T  F  S

## DAY
## 74

- FOLLOW YOUR DIET ○
- TAKE A PROGRESS PHOTO ○
- DRINK 3L WATER EVERYDAY ○
- READ 10 PAGES DAILY ○
- DAILY 45-MINUTE WORKOUT ○

## REFLECTION OF THE DAY

| | |
|---|---|
| **Physical Health** | |
| **Mental Health** | |
| The Things that Made You Feel Good Today | |

## DIET STRATEGY

| | |
|---|---|
| Breakfast | |
| Lunch | |
| Dinner | |
| Snacks | |

## NOTES

## DAILY READING

| BOOK TITEL | |
|---|---|
| AUTHOR | |
| PAGES | |

## WORKOUT PLAN

| WORKOUT PLAN 1 | WORKOUT PLAN 2 |
|---|---|
| | |

# 75 Day Soft Challenge

Date: _____  **S  M  T  W  T  F  S**

**DAY**
**75**

- FOLLOW YOUR DIET ◯
- TAKE A PROGRESS PHOTO ◯
- DRINK 3L WATER EVERYDAY ◯
- READ 10 PAGES DAILY ◯
- DAILY 45-MINUTE WORKOUT ◯

## REFLECTION OF THE DAY

| **Physical Health** | _____ |
| **Mental Health** | _____ |
| **The Things that Made You Feel Good Today** | _____ |

## DIET STRATEGY

| Breakfast | _____ |
| Lunch | _____ |
| Dinner | _____ |
| Snacks | _____ |

## NOTES

## DAILY READING

BOOK TITEL _____
AUTHOR _____
PAGES _____

## WORKOUT PLAN

| WORKOUT PLAN 1 | WORKOUT PLAN 2 |

# 75 Day Soft Challenge

**Date:** _____  **S M T W T F S**

## DAY 76

- FOLLOW YOUR DIET ○
- TAKE A PROGRESS PHOTO ○
- DRINK 3L WATER EVERYDAY ○
- READ 10 PAGES DAILY ○
- DAILY 45-MINUTE WORKOUT ○

## REFLECTION OF THE DAY

**Physical Health** _____

**Mental Health** _____

**The Things that Made You Feel Good Today** _____

## DIET STRATEGY

**Breakfast** _____

**Lunch** _____

**Dinner** _____

**Snacks** _____

## NOTES

## DAILY READING

| BOOK TITEL | |
| AUTHOR | |
| PAGES | |

## WORKOUT PLAN

| WORKOUT PLAN 1 | WORKOUT PLAN 2 |

# 75 Day Soft Challenge

Date: _____     S  M  T  W  T  F  S

## DAY
## 77

- FOLLOW YOUR DIET ⭘
- TAKE A PROGRESS PHOTO ⭘
- DRINK 3L WATER EVERYDAY ⭘
- READ 10 PAGES DAILY ⭘
- DAILY 45-MINUTE WORKOUT ⭘

## REFLECTION OF THE DAY

| Physical Health | _____ |
| Mental Health | _____ |
| The Things that Made You Feel Good Today | _____ |

## DIET STRATEGY

| Breakfast | _____ |
| Lunch | _____ |
| Dinner | _____ |
| Snacks | _____ |

## NOTES

## DAILY READING

BOOK TITEL  _____
AUTHOR  _____
PAGES  _____

## WORKOUT PLAN

WORKOUT PLAN 1     WORKOUT PLAN 2

# 75 Day Soft Challenge

Date: _____    **S  M  T  W  T  F  S**

## DAY
## 78

- FOLLOW YOUR DIET
- TAKE A PROGRESS PHOTO
- DRINK 3L WATER EVERYDAY
- READ 10 PAGES DAILY
- DAILY 45-MINUTE WORKOUT

## REFLECTION OF THE DAY

**Physical Health**

**Mental Health**

**The Things that Made You Feel Good Today**

## DIET STRATEGY

Breakfast

Lunch

Dinner

Snacks

## NOTES

## DAILY READING

BOOK TITEL

AUTHOR

PAGES

## WORKOUT PLAN

WORKOUT PLAN 1

WORKOUT PLAN 2

Made in United States
Troutdale, OR
12/31/2024